I0750328

FINISHING LINE PRESS
www.finishinglinepress.com

Flash Floods
Are Anomalies

poems by

Jesse Morse

Finishing Line Press
Georgetown, Kentucky

Flash Floods Are Anomalies

Originally this book was titled *paragraphs for dolphins [and other anomalies]*. Though that title didn't remain, I would still like to dedicate this book to the coast, any coast, and all you can find there.

let me see
through these borrowed shades a
nice-looking dolphin
—Frank O'Hara, "FROM A DOLPHIN"

ISBN 978-1-64662-542-0 First Edition

ACKNOWLEDGMENTS

Some of these poems originally appeared, in other versions with different titles, in *Greetings, Horse Less Review, Page Boy, and Peaches* and *Bats.*

A great many thanks to Jeffrey Joe Nelson, Jen Tynes, Thomas Walton, and Sam Lohmann, the respective editors.

This little book was written many years ago, and then revisited off and on before arriving here in its current form. I would like to thank W. Scott Howard for his invaluable feedback on this manuscript during one of the periods of revisiting, in late 2014 and early 2015.

Thank you as well to all my poetry teachers, both inside the academy and out, whose numbers are too great to list here.

Publisher: Leah Huete de Maines
Editor: Christen Kincaid
Cover Art: Roosevelt Beach, Grays Harbor County, Washington by Jesse Morse
Author Photo: Rachel Jones, racheljonesartwork.com
Cover Design: Elizabeth Maines McCleavy

Order online: www.finishinglinepress.com
also available on amazon.com

Author inquiries and mail orders:
Finishing Line Press
PO Box 1626
Georgetown, Kentucky 40324
USA

Table of Contents

Wheat,

Pain changes. Pain changes but escapes eternity. Eternally triumphant pain. A robot sings a song. The song of the Lord. Bibliomancy. A bibliomantic robot sings the song of the Lord. Dear robot, I'll call you wheat. Where have all the dolphins gone? Stubborn wheat, to make life in turbulent wind. A district ruled by wind. Dolphins and wind. The inhabitants. The inhabitants of a surf-like district. Surf-like, as in undeniable. Quaint. Built for robots. Ready-made. What is the distance, wheat, from sadness to anger? Vacant to full. Contemplative. Or sinking, dream-like.

Wall,

The parasites of a spring day. Held in constant flux, to attach to a pale green stucco. As suction cups. Embedded in the spaces between rules the shining profligate sun. Don't let it move. Each segment a fugue or a grand sonata. The segue between dreams. As honesty lives. Under a parasol the stem. The blank signing of an idea. A turncoat. Lack. How to build confidence. Like owning a nightmare. Or removal. Dear fight, I'll call you waste. Paint there. End nothing. No thing. Endless gaze, to die on a trapeze. So bounce around. Room.

Dolphin,

Tears in a distance. A vacuum. Dolphins surface in the Great Salt Lake. Fins bent, measured. A perfectly even pace. Dried and cracking skin. An instruction manual to prevent the onslaught of the thought-of future. Cartography the science, the blue and pale veins of leather. Or the fast paced nature of the mind. Restoration. Despite vast numbers, corollary locations, all the dolphins died alone. As in, the recession of the Great Salt Lake. A century's passing. Dear dolphin, I'll call you symptomatic. How this affects the possibilities of engagement. If a curfew means arrival. Once roots take hold. Seeds of aversion fade to obsolete. If the thread runs down the exact center of the curtain how does it affect your ability to float? The impression on a tiny balloon. Up and up.

Downtown,

Pet under dreamt up passages. Midnight's ocean a bridge to the cards of chance. Still, you breathe through gills. How the fading thermometer blue finally dies along the highway. A reservoir over a human body. Leave choice to the outline of its geography. Miles move *a priori.* I wait, then speed speeds. How a bridge out-natures a tree. This return of the self, like fool's gold, a miner blinded by nascent light. A dog. Dear dog, I'll call you purpose. Underlying a trap door. Avarice in the wake of winter. Or summer's howl. Displeased. An exit under a bridge.

Page,

Speckled dots on the reverse open to a longer view. Blankness grows equitable. The idea of equanimity. An abandoned jeep, for example, devoid of rust. Dear page made in a factory, I'll call you libation. The freedom to discredit emptiness. And carry light in a triangle. How a basting lid captures steam. Is it possible to form ephemera? To mould imaginary deaths? Deaths required in attention. And fancy. A battleground. The brain an act of disjointing.

Ball,

As if curves were a replacing. A testimony. Inside a city's firmament, a place. A place to wander, turn up gills. Gills turn up, rather, like the all-angled news. What news, or wonder. Glory. How momentum ends. The energy of a brightly lit ball. Falling. It becomes, in falling, a masterpiece. An attempt at swallowing. How do you block shape? Or personify round? Quick starts, precepts. Deflections on a curb. When the winter contracts, the summer fails. Blessed be. Or else at least to try.

News,

All I hear ascends. Rises in limited destinations. Thrusts then retreats. Panders to unsolved trajectories. Like a baby in a public ceremony. What are a nation's facts? Dear fact, I'll call you direction. Don't die. Know what is needed. A hopeless wandering. Concerted intent. Information moving in a balloon. The opposite of space. As in, how long chemistry matters. The matter of the heart, for instance. A bridge between vision and nesting. To block out the day's ambition. Or rewrite time. Something other than lost. A race car in a square. An explosion.

Factory,

Whatever is made is fake. Like tubes. Dolphins have no use for tubes. Put two and two aside. The way the words unvelop on a page. Made-up aristocracies. See the light the ceremony brings. For freedom. For length upholding. Inside the walls the *ting* of a steel drum. What sacrifice intends. Hues. Microscopic hues on the waves of the city's night. Go home. After work go home. Then pilot the dark. The appearance of veins through skin. Through fur. Mammals made in a factory. Dear then, I'll call you now. Troubles. No troubles.

Upholding,

Continued in the distant spacing an interval to upset time. An orange springtime. A stereo. Notwithstanding any ethics. Nor forward movement. The logic of revenge, for instance, overwhelmed by clouds, music. Clouds adrift at what register. A legal battle. Given thought on to paper. How difference weighs a customer's mind. Unnecessary upholding, I'll call you blanket. How does logic stay warm? Ambition, drive. Unread manuals in an empty prairie. Wind winds. Houses fall. Like death a signature. Copy. Photocopy. Fake plastic trees, or organs. Learn, again, to run.

Fantastic,

Realignment vs. rearrangement. For reward. For dreams. In pattering anticipation. A wide open sea. Revisit the way a house is built, like a city made of mushroom. A white open pistol. Dear pistol, I'll call you fracture. Like edging. What power believes. Fire alone in a quarter. A vacuum suffering. On philanthropy: adjust. Intoxicating beauty, enough on its own. Like mist, lifting. Stay. Or leave, return. As history's realm, re-written for religious exposition. Insight's dark play, a theatre for topography.

Jet Plane,

Fly. That flies. Last in a generation's method of achievement. To underwrite the future's ill logic. All the dolphins flown in saltwater crafts. To where? Where does fever go? Enclosed by cumbrance. The wheezing olla brain. Or leans. Brain-lean. Like a root vegetable, mashed for soup. Anaplastic hum. The air there. The practical act of looking back. Time's slipstream. Dear slipstream, I'll call you come what may. No matter the expectations, loss lingers. Like retrieval. How presence gets felt in memory shards. Ice picks. Drinks. At play in epistemology. Moving back to front. Up above and going over. Desalted by spheres and freezing wind.

Colloquial,

Would we even get along? Grandstand. To put up or bleacher. An actress. A canyon made of chutes. An unnavigable dolphin-thought. There. How maps set. Or sit. To wait. How time becomes a geometry. Dear dolphin-thought, I'll call you tactile. How not to skate around but force awkwardness. Why weird. Weird beard. Or fear. A fear of words. Head descending. Honesty's stop-gap submissive in accomplishment. Tired nature. To get picked up. Detailed in war. Or a citizen express. Hard to follow in the expanse of normal. Blitz to weary or dull over time.

Architecture,

Come what may says never ending. Expanding and expanding. How to arrive in a graceful light. Or stretch. Control-less. Muscle. The image of becoming a threat. Like fabric, infrastructure. The plot's master plan. Finite's impossibility to venture proximity. Or government product. Spired to the dreary rain. As a blueprint of the past. A vertical line, curved. When does thought become problematic? Dear architecture, I'll call you medicine. A passage for the dead, bundled in kindling. Erect in its tragedy. All consequence inconsequential. All thought despotic.

Syllepsis,

Lips, puckered. Onomatopoeia. A mourning. An aged blanket in ability. Like a poem. Any poem. Any poem unable. How to distinguish tailings given a denizen. Any denizen. To drip-dry the outcome of a tornado. Shaped as a welcome mat. To exit logic. Dear intent, I'll call you flash flood. Like an empty water bowl. How to write seasons in reverse. An anchored journey. Adrift at sea. Incapable of sensation. Like finding where balloons land. Ideally an emblem. A moment, taken, in lieu of hiding. As sweet as honey. Past, yet loved. Rather wooed. Apitch.

Onomatopoeia,

Sounds. Sounds in a steel. Maids. Tea kettle ettle ettle. The following of an invisible flicker. A vertical crawl. Trapeze. To retire an arrow. Or arch, rather. A trajectory to die by. The sound there. Bullet-like yet insensate. Drafted on truth. As principle behind a shaded honor. A bride. Or border-less. Cemented from the ground up. Apposite. A luxurious bus. Dear meaning, I'll call you engendered. Like plosives, labials. Then the other. Whatever is relative makes good. Or God, even. Couples at play in gibberish. To air out the mouth. Holes. Holy.

God,

A fire engine, gotten under. Like methodology. How do you end desire? A ringing phone. Or not. Like tin cans bracketing a string. As in, bridging a rush in winter's tradition. A highlight film. Turniped. Cartwheels in a wind tunnel. Human flight, rooftops. Eject through television. How belief fosters movement. The physical act or interplay. Like northern eyes. Dear unattainable, I'll call you squeezed. As in hoped for. A place to figure in. Like exegesis. Unattainable gone fly. Reverence a palace for the weary. An emergency exit. Easy answers. To die, live. Whatever is gained is kept. How to know? A shrine I suppose. Artifact.

Span,

A coterie. Or fresh wounds. The belief in realization. Like ascension. What's looked toward. The lack of female distance. How posturing gets reconciled, for instance. The language of an ex-patriot. Miscalculations. On top of living like pretending what's near. Or smoke. How narratives twist. A diamond-like plan for our making. Though no. Insouciant, our acting, in its waiting. How to feign compromise? Make embetterment full. Dear misjudged, I'll call you apparition. A ghost unmade making. Worth-less. Unclear. As point A to point B. Or a cue-less in-between. To dream in ancestry. Ingested voices, negated. Imprecise precision. Span left falling.

Chop,

Verbs, nouns and articles on the inside. Extracted like sentences but begun again. Toward vision and segment. Or attempts at vernacular. Word-dreams. How to, simply, say what you mean? A frozen waterfall. Sound's absence. The performed pain there. A performance on pain. Or painting, rather. Dear painting, I'll call you foreign. Thus subdued. As in, under-human. Flowless. History's notebook a firmament in acquired taste. So stir, wrangle. Nothing had in vacant malaise. Like an invisibly panicked proprietor. Night's sublimation. Chop wracked on chains. Frighted. Or flickering. As creatures make love. Unforetold, the frost. Trailed in its bending.

Dust,

Ask it, yourself the bright red earth. Platitudes. How laundry spins. As whirls wind. Unexplored caverns. Breathless rock, as in heretofore unremarkable. Dull intent once revealed. Disobedient isotopes. Like a murder on a train. Even dolphin-like. Or whaled, rather. Beached. How long 'til the tapestry disintegrates? Windowsill. To build venture, like snapshots of tracks. Make play at christening. In memory. Image-less. The thinning of soap. Dear past, I'll call you severed. Uncomfortable. As in, baited, hook-less. Like adjusting to decay. Or the stenographer's dust crumbled letters. How to love from the ground up? A whim. Dressed up but reeling. Twitching.

Integrated,

Bring the faithful maps. Another country's calibration. Like snorkeling the foreign consistency of a daydream. How planets delineate. Unkempt, this bragging. Inside a flower an answer. Like entering a nation's irascible movement. How to chart a blistering people? As in, the sun's stubborn recalcitrance. Or eternity's demeanor. Life's decisions on prosper. To blend part radical, part square. Dear disintegrated, I'll call you parked. As rodent-run or ladder-scurry. Twist. A filtering through politic. Uselessly drunk on phantoms. Like a farm of implausible suggestions harvested for usury. Nowhere to turn in argument's gaze. Fear-driven. Insensate. As in, no sense. Ever more to try.

Filtering,

Ablaze. Ablaze in a barnstorm. Abandoned. The opera light of the Midwest. Or under the high definition sea. Chiaroscuro. Formal-less. Constructed in tones. Released in spasm and electricity. Crippled. At bay, rather. Adrift in an anchored display. A child's twilit diorama. To just barely fit. So interred. Wash through into stuck. Severed predisposition. What are memory's limits? A polished stone, for instance, awash in its river. Finned. To overwinter without though moving through. Or carving. Dear carving, I'll call you deadened. Verve-less. A pigeon. Where to go to die? Mummified streets. As anyone. An attempt at dressing.

Claustrophobia,

Universal but specific to. Children walking. A thing desired never taken. As space, forgotten. Laughing in buttons. Road-blocked. Passed up for false accounting. Society's farts, for instance. How planes burgeon. A smoothness. Sheltered, bereaved. Clotted inside plastic. Spaced as blood. How to become new? A trapdoor to discard the dead. Or posit. Dear policeman, I'll call you budged. Gender-specific. Identity's tornado a flood, a blessing on drafting. How a thief pilfers the night's vicissitudes. This distant dreaming. Trapped then simply over. Removed in succession. Recalled, rather. To reclaim spirit. Contracting out a blotted screen. Light-less. Yet pulsing, steady.

Policeman,

Impossibility a sponge, as in absorbent. Poverty's play. Like a bludgeoning of drastic undertakings. Acamp in the desert. Or putrefaction. To eliminate a nation's wasteful theories. Distress signal. Authority's glance on failure. So skittish. Dear obeisance, I'll call you covered in fur. Gland-like. Sweated. A possible outcome. In need of ostentation. How waiting gets plausible. Hurry-less. Just at bay. Oh officer. Oh dolphin. A summer fade on the jagged horizon. To exit realm in principal. Vicarious pleasantries. Man-made and bleached. Fast temperature. Emaciate. How a symphony ends. Or satiate. What makes the world full? In lieu of quietude. A possible stance. Emphatic or unwilling. As in, opposed. Wall-like.

Jade(d),

Handcuffs. The past in stone. Like parliament. Petals, drooped then fallen. Askew. Insight's rotten declarations. Perceived as such, taken. To falter in crisis. Then parsimonious. Repeat. Dear such, I'll call you x'd. Failed so buried, darkened. As rain draws wind. As advice. Prophet-less. Profiteering, rather. In surplus of light. What's not needed so thrown. To vet method's arbitrations. Like broken plays. Spindled past. Consummate. Uncharted acquaintance. Greened or blaspheme. A prisoner's love, for instance. How to continue to continue? A perplexed sealant. In sequence. Or not. Just curled, bereaved. Complete. Naked in longing. Absent, ever absent.

Posit,

Ively. Or lively, rather. To get beasted anew. Beset, rather. How an invitation empties. Or a leaf pinks. Hope's daily recurrence. Like an icy phantasm. The skinny. Depth's register, parted by vacuum. The serpent-like definition of an outline. A slant of sunlight, for instance. Dear poem, I'll call you taxonomy. So pleased. As in, following. Palliated. Gone pixel. Like a compromised wind-stop. Eager to reckon sideways or make haste in belonging. Saturate. Apropos. How no trial is equal. Belief-less. Bare, though encrusted. So hostile. Swamped out of fathom. Left guessing on nerves. Aloft yet somehow below. Ashake. Apiled. Blown.

Left Guessing,

A matter of presentation in a cold passage. Like dessert. Or contemplation. Once in doubt now vacant. Like water. How breath particulates or destinations expire. An aster. Pistol for change. What morning brings. Play-less. Malfeasance. As in, room-less. How the unsituated future talks. For what? Dear unreturnable, I'll call you supple. Primary. Attained sequentially yet startled. Like an exploding bridge. Looted. Or luted. As in, mythology. Delivered in foreign constitution. A line's acceptance. Or erasure's premeditation. A television in reverse. Comfort's contract. Like a rough draft of an abacus. The poet's tendency to count. What wonder. Grasped at then left, observed.

Abacus,

Hopeless, perhaps, when the past ends. On a pogo stick. Forgotten. Pensively dreamt but sacrificed. To realize a plot-less plot. How the vertical outweighs what it's held for. Costumed, so vulnerable. Fence-less. Though counting. Always counting. Dear mystery, I'll call you waited for. Intended though never appropriated. Hopscotched, rather. Made uniform. How culture critiques the blessed. So fast forward. At what point do dreams stunt growth? Glistening. Close to a smile. To kidnap preferential distance. Taken as leaves fall. In chalk. External. Pardoned toward bone. Rather-less.

Deter,

Named. As in, misunderstood. Unaccomplished so removed though fought over. As a waterwheel turns in absentia. Or cement sets. Like failing at jump rope. Penniless. Yet cajoled. Taunted then made reverent. Like fireworks. Where do they fall once blown? Haphazard earth. Unwilling to lie in debt. Pushed forward as standard issue. Enterprised on marriage's whistle. An attempt at rising. Dried on loan. Forlorned. Dear miscarriage, I'll call you inconceivable. Tack-blasted. Goal-less. As in, sent without fortitude. Incognito's interminable sleep. Like living in misguided pursuit. Still round and lit-up. Without favor nor fervor. To undo remorse. Or make safe. Fought for then gone.

Traction,

Hope spins outside desire. Like bravery, made. Fastened. A falling time-piece. As in, nothing remembered gets excavated. Whether for family. Or history's monocle. Its piercing pince-nez. Like perfection's rise and dip. A dolphin fin. Meditations in an emergence. How combat makes apathy. Dear newness, I'll call you separated. As in, keeping. Or plastic. The blood-life of tangential thinking. Diagrams halfway to full or frozen. Stuck by momentum. Alcohol's problem. When does clarity avail itself? So chosen incorrectly to maintain rapport. Politeness overrated. Fault-less. As in, without traction. Planted and spinning. Policed. Garnered out of. Made sequential in regards to where a rainbow touches. Fostered, then. Aground. Though looking. Always looking.

Part Way,

White and brown circles then black. Dusted. Run out or off. Unskilled in believing. Now bleeding. As in, penned. Caged, rather. To emerge from a dark box with splatter-vision. Church-like. How an alien feels in wagging. To arrive there in fact. Beleaguered in exposition. Thought-less. An attempt at going. Pasture's nativity. Or sand-castles. Mud's purification. How the wind lends desperation. Or visibility. What, in fact, makes fact possible? Talent's deposition. Unused. Disabused even. Weighted. Bred to dream in part. Like burnt hair. The call of centering affected, obstacled. Fired up as an arrow through velvet. Stench-less. Situated in drastic measure. Dear drastic, I'll call you sensed. As duress. Holy modal, perhaps. Unrealized, how thought sculpts its person. How time molds stiff.

Permission Slip,

Relapse's web planted through constellation and faculty. The seed night (p)lays, for instance, whipped into growing. What access allows. Separation's final lock. Keyed or key-less. Like tunnel vision. Draped in modest assumption. Filched, then tethered. How destiny dies then tassels out. To eliminate each day's expectation. Earth-less. Laid under in resumption. Plowed for future calligraphy. Out-plowed, even. Dear announcement, I'll call you every little thing. Analysis's tragedy like magical thinking. What's been per missed in alteration. Unruly or ruled. Living forged through a box. A martyr complex. A death lost in fascination. Culpability excused in its wavering absence. Ambition, complacence. Dimly felt. Forgotten, glossed or subsumed.

Gigantic,

Not really friendly. Though the opposite of parsed. Over-salted, even. Fruit-less. To live out presumption's avarice. Or jet-lag's disinterest. As in, the underdog. Uprooted then rooted for. At last given into. Ripped, parted, dreamt afoot. Or afloat. To gaze down on the imagined future. An empty silo, for instance, as a postcard for therapy. Dear therapy, I'll call you therapy. Though huge, distrustful. Thunder-catted. Drawn towards creation's quest for search. Alighted in color's absence. How would dreams act given dominion? A passageway for firmaments. Conquistadored. Like old charts. Ablown. Opened out to hide.

Burst,

To minister the inside of cells. Shot through as video, grained. Parlayed. How fruit grows, falls. Traps reseeded. Like sun-blistered skin. Or the physical nature of fat. White, bubbled. To pass at face value. Or face anxiety's salutations as tides recede. Like poetry's possibilities. Delineated. Dream-dead. Precipice-less. How is nakedness reflected? Mirrored. Dear mirror, I'll call you ringed. Terrored in. Brought forward but kept at bay. Transfigured, then falsely scintillated. Disallowed due to vacuum. Crookedness-less. Cartooned. A draft to honor honor by. Though villainous. Lodged in deceit and ardor. So ran from. Fleeced or fled. Agogged. Left down.

Kept At Bay,

Bollixed. The ringing ears cut through in attachment's haze. As atrophy. Twined in danger's landscape. What follows. To break out of birth's sac. Yet immobile. Like a theatre fire. An unpainted pew. How rows of seats hum. Cabin-chucked. Though able to play. Dear play, I'll call you circumstantial. Ungummed, revolving. Listenable made bare in isolation. Sand-scraped. What's not gotten into despite the dolling up. How the future allays unlike optometries. As remotely tethered. To see through a kicking. Or a plastered map in relief. Pleasant, sagging. How fashionable opportunity becomes. Longing stunted. How do we ascertain our dreams? Are they lost in movement? Petrified emotion. Fog-creep. What's bled in consternation availed. Perched, blessing. A muted soundscape.

Art,

How to abide in your shadow? Time after time to wait. Tears. Or foreign singing. Tongue-like and present. Shaded in outline. Hued. Who'd even. Bunkered in a war-less topography. Having to color asphalt. Primary. To seed meaning. Though unable to plant. Twang-like. A basement. Dear voice, I'll call you matter. So brought. Tabled now. Framed as molded consequence. Eaten, quenched. Blood-colored. As in, living in purpose. Dream-less. Apaint. Tire's movement. Or steeple's faith. Thus twisted. Like pacing on stilts. Trusted in, fancied. Yet purloined, fashioned after. Poverty-less. The state's misguided requirements. When do art and life separate? Dear dolphin, I'll call you poem. Once afloat. Now entrenched. Dressed for. Living in.

Jesse Morse holds a poetry PhD from University of Denver. He is currently a faculty member at Clark College in Vancouver, WA. His poems and book reviews have appeared in *Amerarcana, Bombay Gin, Colorado Review, Denver Quarterly, Golden Handcuffs Review, jacketmagazine, Page Boy, Poetry Flash,* and *Vanitas*, among others. He reviews sports literature for *Oregon Sports News.* His chapbook—*Rotations* (part of the Eric Chavez Sonnets)—was once published by C_L Press. He plays guitar and sings in the rock band The Whirlies (https://thewhirlies.bandcamp.com/releases), and helps run 1122 Gallery (https://1122gallery.com/index.html) in Portland, Oregon, where he lives with his wife, the poet Jennifer Denrow, and their daughter Wren.

www.ingramcontent.com/pod-product-compliance
Lightning Source LLC
LaVergne TN
LVHW051022080826
845145LV00009B/2755

* 9 7 8 1 6 4 6 6 2 5 4 2 0 *